I Am Not In A Good Place

~~Poems~~
**A cry for help by
Derek Porterfield**

Copyright © 2022 by Derek Porterfield
All rights reserved
No part of this book may be reproduced in any form or by any electronic or mechanical means, including information storage and retrieval systems, without written permission from the author, except for the use of brief quotations in a book review.

Published by TNDMTR Publishing a division of TNDMTR

Visit our website at TNDMTR.COM

First published in 2022

Any similarity to real people, living or dead is not intentional and is purely coincidence. Except for you. That's right. You know who you are, Frank.

ISBN 978-1-7370305-1-5

Printed in the United States of America

This book is dedicated to all of the people that supported the Kick-Starter. You made this possible and inflated my already ridiculous ego. Thank you.

I AM NOT IN A GOOD PLACE

Contents

The Good Place	10
IN WAYS PROFOUND AND ETERNAL	13
AYE! ME	14
CHEMICAL DEPENDENCY	15
MISS ERA BLEHHHH	16
LIGHT LEAKS	17
LOUD SONGS AND BAD HEARING	18
THINGS I LOVE	19
KISSING	21
LISTING	22
SONGS AND BOOKS	23
TEXTS FROM MY BEST FRIEND	24
I DID THE MATH	25
PRACTICING	30
TRUCKS AND STUFF	31
MATH STUFF	32
TOO MANY POEMS	33
ATTRACTION SHIFT	34
DEVILED DETAILS	35
YOU LIKE JOE	36
FLING ME	37
SECOND STRING	38
WHISPER	39
CUT THIS MELODRAMATIC BULLSHIT	40
YOU DON'T LOVE ME	41
EXTROPICAL THUNDER	42
LDR	43
NOT A FAN	44
SAME	45
APEROL SPRITZ AND OTHER POUR JOKES	46
HIRAETH	47
LAST RITES	48
CHANGE	49
PERFECT DAY	50
APATHY STUFF	51
ACCOUNTANT	54
THE DREAM	55
I'M LONELY	56
CIGARETTES AND SAINTS	57
ALL GODS ARE THE SAME	58

OVER INVESTED	**59**
ARMCHAIREGGEDON	**60**
SETTLE DOWN	**61**
CAN'T C	**62**
DAMN	**63**
YOU LIE PRETTY	**64**
NICKI MENAGE	**65**
LAKE LOVE	**66**
HOT GIRLS ON THE INTERNET	**67**
STONES AND SHARP EDGES	**68**
I AM BLISSFUL	**69**
DOCTOR THUNDER	**70**
READ THIS ONE DUMBASS	**71**
METH TOWN BOMB CITY HOMETOWN SO SHITTY	**72**
MEN WILL LITERALLY GO TO THERAPY	**73**
QUIRKY	**74**
THE STRANGULATION OF THE BISHOP	**75**
COLORFUL	**76**
PSL	**77**
PRIORITY	**78**
RUDYARD KIPLING SHIT	**79**
UNDONE	**80**
DECEMBER BIRTHDAYS	**81**
YOU SHOULD SIMILE MORE	**82**
NYQUIL	**83**
UNHAPPY	**84**
DAFT PUNK	**85**
STAR TREK REFERENCE	**86**
CHARON and KAREN	**87**
DOWN DOWN BABY	**88**
HOLDING HANDS	**89**
DON'T FIGHT THIS FIRE	**90**
ADVICE	**91**
NO CAP	**92**
DAUGHTER	**93**
RUPI WHO	**94**
MOURNING COFFEE	**96**
BOYFRIEND MATERIALS	**97**
Lovely	**98**
Jeremy Bearimy	**101**

TARYN	**104**
MACHELLE	**106**
THEATER WEIRD	**107**
ANDREW MONROE	**108**
CHRISTIAN	**110**
MORGAN	**112**
CARTER	**114**
JANSEN	**115**
HADLEE	**116**
TALON	**117**
MIMI & PAWPAW	**119**
TYLER & BETHANY	**120**
RACHAEL	**122**
TEYSHA & MATT	**124**
ANDREW BRANDT	**126**
The Bad Place	**127**
UNREQUITED	**128**
THIRTY- THREE	**131**
FATHER'S DAY	**134**
WALK	**137**
EMERGENCY	**141**
INTENTIONED	**145**
THANKS	**150**
LEAVE A REVIEW	**154**

I Am Not In A Good Place

The Good Place

  I was naive. Or hopeful? It's in a strange space between the two that I choose to exist romantically. She was out of my league, which is a much more appropriate metaphor than is altogether funny. Her smile still startles me from sleeping around 4am. It's been that way for a few weeks now.
But naivety and hope both leave us vulnerable. And isn't that the point? To find someone in whose company we can allow ourselves to be hurt? To find respite in the arms of another human who allows you a moment of weakness in a life of impossibly constant performance.
I found that.
And it was nice.
She was nice.
I traveled around with her. A mistake with something impermanent, as those places now echo endlessly of shared experience and missed possibilities.
And God damn she could kiss. I mean, first kisses are al-

ways great, right? Full of highschool hormones and nerves acting as fireworks all along our insides.
But this first kiss…man, it was different. For me at least. Storybook, sounds too renaissance for my taste, so let's just say that the first kiss was stolen from a coming of age movie written in the early 2000s. A girl and a boy to whom the universe, through no small twists of luck and fate, decided to show kindness. I won't describe it here. My words would muddy the truth of it and besides, it was ours, and not something I want to share.
As so many things do, her interest or investment waned and I was left with a self reflective unhappiness.
I don't know how to do this stuff. And at this point, it could be argued that I'm the problem, right? I'm nearing 34 at the time of writing this. I'll be ~~34~~ 35 when it comes out and I'm wrestling with the same questions anyone stumbling through love and relationships in this strange new era of dating is asking.
What am I missing?
What's wrong with me?
Why are Becky and Judas still trying to get me to be a part of that pyramid scheme?
The usual junk.
I miss the girl. Writing is a sort of trauma response I guess, so I'll be bleeding into a new project by way of distraction and hopefully at the end I'll have something worth sharing with anyone who may be having their own moment of self hatred and heartache.
I thought for a very large portion of my life that we could mold our own happiness into the shape of a story that we write with others. I realize now that there isn't really a story that any of us can reliably narrate. The world is too full of unpredictability, the universe too wild, her ex-boyfriend too regularly blowing up her phone and asking her

to dinner.

But it's within that chaos that we can discover the tragic art of experience. And though it's been exhausting, I'm doing my best to see it that way. A painting in a house that I'm merely visiting while waiting out the storm. There's another house, another city, another new range of wonderful, and fantastic and lovely and terrible feelings to discover. Most of them are kinda rough. But that's what makes those moments of internal fireworks feel so profound. And I'm good with that. I hope you dig the things I wrote on my way to chasing something resembling peace and I hope that you find your own. Cause you are worth all of the romantic joy you've yet to find. And I probably love you.

I absolutely loved her.

5...
4...
4...
3...
2...
1...

Go

IN WAYS PROFOUND AND ETERNAL

I love you
In ways profound and eternal
I love you
With reason and not condition
With hope
And not restriction
With longing
Not lust
…
Okay a little lust
But see, for you my heart is an amalgam
Of love, lust, longing, and libation
Libation to the point of intoxication
I'm waiting and wishing and yes, even praying
A rare thing for me
That you return all the feelings I've tossed out to the ether
In hopes that souls really do speak to each other
Cause I believe
In the saccharine sweet songs of saints that say
Ours
Our souls
Were mates

AYE! ME

The very first gift I bought for a girl
Was Smashing Pumpkins - Siamese dreams
I bought it at the mall at an FYE
She liked that record but
She didn't like me

CHEMICAL DEPENDENCY

I'm just chasing dopamine
The chemical bump that we all need
That wave of happy in the wake of a storm
A blanket on cold nights to keep me warm
But brain waves are hard to catch
I'm trying, but honest, not giving it my best
And in those dark moments
Absent of serotonin
I think I'll give up chasing
Maybe this time I'll see if the dopamine will chase me

MISS ERA BLEHHHH

Yea I'm fuckin miserable
Can't seem to get you back
You've got your own life babe
I promise that I get that
But we could share Netflix logins
Baskin robbins and each other's beds
Cause I still spend my nights faded hoping that you smile when you read my texts
Just another bad meme or a joke about wishing I was dead
What happens next?
Yea I'm fucking miserable
It's different now that you left
Wrote a new book though
So I guess that I've got that
But there's a thread still pulling my heart apart
Towards wherever you wind up next
Blurring you out with alcohol
In sports bars placing bets
On another bad team for a new girl in my bed
What happens next

LIGHT LEAKS

You were shattered and remade yourself whole
The fractures leaking light from the center of your soul
A light that if not for the breaks would be unseen
How beautiful,
How lovely,
Our emotional baggage can be.
And within the light leaks our film was exposed
Unintended consequence of mixing highs and lows
You were patient and kind, yet careful too
I was reckless in my endless pursuit of you
And that photograph of romance was made more striking by the light
Like the orange white flames licking soft at our sides
We were burning in the moments shared all in blue
Fractured, reckless, perfect, you.

LOUD SONGS AND BAD HEARING

You're all of my favorite hits of dopamine
I turn the music up until it hurts me
Not quite as badly as I hurt me
Not quite as deeply
But close
I drive faster than I ought to
Like I used to
Not quite reckless
Almost
Not quite alive
But I'm close

THINGS I LOVE

I love long walks during sunset with a podcast on my headphones
I love quiet cooking in the evening with wine while I'm alone
I love the sound of my daughter laughing while chasing our dog through the house
I love the feeling of accomplishment after conquering my ever present doubts
The sound of leaves under your feet when walking in early fall
The taste of coffee and chocolate and cool mornings and mockingbird songs
The way it feels when you hold hands for the first time
The smell of her perfume when the wind blows just right
The taste of her lips when I was still nervous to kiss them
And the way that our hearts seem to suddenly change rhythm
I love the road trips you don't plan
The ramen restaurants in movies about Japan
The way the world feels more romantic late at night
I love the color of every girl's eyes
I think it's really just the girls that I like
But I love the glimmer that's inside
Before something within us fades
I love the way we bathe in a constant stream of misery
But everyday choose to move on willingly
There's something absolutely inspiring about that
Don't you think?
I love good wine
I love music and crunchy guitar tones
I love quietly watching my friends achieve all of their goals
I love movies in empty theaters

I love walking in soft rain
I love doing the things a younger me would have considered fucking insane
I love reading a good book on those rare, perfect days,
I love the smell of baked bread, especially homemade
I love comedy clubs in foreign towns
Parents that were parents when mine weren't around
The drop in your stomach as the rollercoaster is just beginning to fall
The shared joy of good food and strong alcohol
The chills after discovering and writing a decent tune
But more than all of it
I
Love
You

KISSING

I admit
There were so many times that I kissed you with my eyes open to see
I wanted to remember the way you looked so close to me
Both of us happy
No burden to carry
Even then I guess I knew you were temporary

LISTING

You are golden hour
You are subtle harmonic notes
You are the feeling a heart makes when you first take off your clothes
You are empty beaches and quiet laughter
Because you are everything lovely and tacit
But now
You are the itch in my eye
The migraine at night
The tired metaphor of a phantom limb
Cliches like you
Preferring songs written by him
Empty from messages sent and left read
Because I can't get you the fuck out of my head

SONGS AND BOOKS

I don't stay friends with my exes
Cause they all end up in my music
If I have heartbreak I'm gonna use it
And if I go on one more bad first date I might lose it
I don't stay friend with my exes
Probably cause I'm the problem
Or when they had their own I wanted to solve em
When she just wanted an ear and some company
I guess it's just part of getting older
Finding pieces of your heart moved to your shoulder
And when the blood that's on my sleeve
Falls onto your white shirt
I'll apologize for stealing lines from Taking Back Sunday
co-opted for my own hurt
And never growing up past highschool
You and me
Could be closer but you probably see
I'm just sitting, anxiously anticipating
The song you'll someday be

TEXTS FROM MY BEST FRIEND

"Bro I think this might be what love feels like"
NARRATOR: (it wasn't)

I DID THE MATH

I did the math
The odds
On running into you again after three years of avoidance.
I did the math
Cause in my head that seems impossible.
The probability of seeing you
But I mean
There's only 198,955 people in Amarillo
Give or take
Someone might die
Or have a baby today
So Like 198,950 something
And you were there
At the EXACT same time as me in an aisle in a store looking for shit neither of us really needs
I did the math
There's 24 hours in a day
And of that there's only like 16 or 17 anyone is really awake
And that store is only open 14 of those waking hours
And most people work at least a few of those hours
But there you were
It was like 3
And you looked up from your phone and saw me
I did the math
Your parents live in Canyon, and your ex fiance lived pretty close
So maybe we add the people that make up both of those?
That's 15,305 people added to those 198,950 something
I mean that has to account for something
That the two of us were in the same exact spot at a time when you weren't with someone
I mean like *with* someone
Single I guess

Cause I was single too
That's not just coincidence
Right?
I did the math
I mean, Google helped me a bit
I sorted the numbers into charts in excel and shit
And I found out that each of us is floating on a rock
Deep in space
At a speed that feels like such a slow pace
But in space
That hurling hunk of hubris is balancing just right
That it allowed a couple bacteria to smash and make life
and that life kept making more life
Until we finally evolved
A bunch of gross, knuckle dragging, neanderthals
Discovering
That there's more than just the smashing of genitalia
You could care for and even *love* the other humanoid mammalia
But they didn't call it love they just grunted and muttered
The kind of grunt that whispers
I want her more than all the others
So those neanderthals, right?
They started making homes and built villages and tools and
I imagine one of them cut their hair pretty cool
If I'd met you then, bereft of wordplay and generational facial symmetry,
I think the odds wouldn't have been quite as crazy
Maybe
I think with less humans you stick close to your community
So it's way more likely of you running into me
I don't know, just kinda thinking through things

But that village got into some scuffles
Maybe the one with a cool haircut died
And maybe they kept meandering through the maze that we begrudgingly call life
Maybe they find another village, and the people there were kinda cool
So they combined and made cities and helped each other with their tools
That's a pretty remarkable thing.
In fact all life is contingent upon that wildly low probability
Of those prehistoric families combining forces to stay relevant
And then
THEN!
They keep growing the tribe
Like some girl took over the hunting and a dude says "That's my wife"
They invented a whole custom, finding upshots in monogamy
Living with some safety and raising family in harmony
And that romance that they had discovered so very long ago
Became the tenant upon which they began to build homes
And so it goes, to steal a phrase,
They grow
I'm not that great with history and I know this is long winded I'll do my best to build a summary
A bunch of things kept happening
Some dude in some city invents cool technology
And we catch up to the modern 21st century
I know, I know, I'm skipping a few things
But neanderthals to kings
Kings through to pilgrims

Pilgrims evolving or perhaps devolving into the giant tech conglomerates developing computing
You playing on phone built off of that computing
Honestly
It's alarming
We
Shouldn't even exist
But we
Thanks to those horny bacteria back a bajillion fucking centuries
Are standing in the very same place, you see?
I did the math
The odds of you
Perfect as ever with hair darker than I remembered
And a smile that stopped my heart beat for only that split second
Before I captured the words I thought would be charming
Hoping to god you wouldn't find me alarmingly
Forward
And there you were
The odds of that are absurd
This is how the math works
Clandestined mathematics, check this out
In a city of like 200,000 something people
In a world of 8 billion
On rock that sits just perfectly in space to support the type of lungs that we use to breathe
Those hearts that we feel beat
The brains I know sync
To each other in a way that can only be described when free of the confines
Of science, and math and reason
We were there not by chance
Or equation

Nor by any algorithm
There isn't single statistical reason I could manage to work out
You were there
And I believe this
Because the whole universe conspires to give you what you want
I read that once
You are everything I've chased in shitty poems and bad midwestern emo music
You have a kindness and a passion and an intelligent resolve
You're the hottest woman on this earth and I feel like I've seen enough to compare them all
You're everything beautiful
and
I got that second chance
What
Are
The odds
The mathematical probability?
I did the math
And still fucked up that impossibly rare opportunity
I did the math
And lightning struck twice
and still I'm not wise
Enough
to keep you

PRACTICING

If I'm being honest
I think I'll end up on my own
I don't even think I can blame it
On a deficiency of testosterone
Could you really condemn
The ones that leave and don't come back
I think that it's me now
I understand that the deck is stacked
I'll just remove this facade
I thought sincerely I hated you but really I hated God
I'm not worth the effort of it all
I can't fix the problem
With a surplus of alcohol
I'm doing my best though
Blurred eyes making you more pretty
I'm doing my best now
I swear before was just practicing

TRUCKS AND STUFF

I love you like country music
As the world is on fire
Songs about branded beer
And muddy truck tires
And women full of patriotic cheer
But
God damn the red white and blue
Cause I hate country music
Almost as much as I hate you

MATH STUFF

There were a billion eternities in which we never ran into each other
But in this one I found you
Even if only for the equivalent of a shallow breath
Even if it was a fraction of what I hoped it could be
I found you
And for that
This lifetime was shaped ever so much more perfectly

TOO MANY POEMS

I recognized your hands
In the picture of the book that I gave you
Only way I see you now is on the page for my shitty poetry reviews
Oh but we had fire once
Oh we were something else
Tried to find some words or grand gesture that could help
Nothing seems to help
I couldn't help…

But recognize your blanket
I think I helped you fold it once
Now I'm wondering all the time if you're under it
Holding hands and calling it love
Oh but we could have
Should have
I don't want to be too bold
I just saw your hands
My mind just ran
Possibilities and foolish hope

ATTRACTION SHIFT

I'm not saying that it's the worst part
It probably isn't
I'm not even gonna claim it's top ten
But the fact that I dated you
And that shit made me feel
Attracted to blondes
Is bullshit

DEVILED DETAILS

If the devil is in the details
it means that god is in the broad strokes
And you and I are somewhere in between both of those
Your clothes
On the floor of our hotel room
Your eyes locked steady with mine
Those may be the details
But I'm more interested in the timeline
Broad though it may be
I wanted you with me
And got lost with the devil and I'm cursing at god
For the space we left in between
You: the God
And the devil is me

YOU LIKE JOE

I don't know what love is
I've flirted with it a time or two
Found it's outer edges
And mistook them for you
I don't know what love is
I stay ever more confused
When crossing paths with its likeness
But never finding it reflected in you

FLING ME

I tend to be the fling
Before she finds the real thing
The last bang before her last hang
The one she explores before closing the doors to everyone
but her someone
I feel like Nick Miller
Good Luck Chuck
The one you like
But just don't love
The guy you dig but only want to fuck
The dude that's fun but would just hold you up

SECOND STRING

I'm a backup
A second string
But more like a tampon than a sports team
Something you throw out
Something you don't need
You already have the first string

WHISPER

It was a lovers whisper
Soft
Meant only for you
As though the weight of concentration might break its message
And so you barely acknowledge it
You don't move
So as not to disturb unspoken, loving truths

Derek Porterfield

CUT THIS MELODRAMATIC BULLSHIT

YOU DON'T LOVE ME

You don't love me
I'm just present in ways your father wasn't
I just hug you tighter than your mom did
You don't even like me
You like feeling wanted
And so I'll serve as mud in your sieve
Holding water and pretending that we want to live
In each other's half adoring company just long enough to
die
With someone, whoever, literally anyone
By our side

EXTROPICAL THUNDER

They say that the entire universe is in a constant state of extropy
Exploding outwards towards endless infinities
A boundless expanse towards the unknown
An observable piece of the explosion that started us
That outward growth is in our nature
Baked somewhere deep within our DNA
Because it is nature itself
To explode
I think maybe that's why I'm so uneasy
So violently far from peace
Because after you
I'm collapsing
Inward
My existence a combat of
Extropic entropy

LDR

You felt like fall mornings and hot coffee
Like the warmth in John Legend's voice
You smelled of something beautiful
I assume
I can't smell and neither can you
Each of us anosmic and you, probably blind
I've got mirrors in my house
I know I'm not worth your time
And I see you
All resplendent and wonderful
And I see me
A Midwest mistake in a t-shirt and jeans
I should have been more cautious
I could have been more reserved
But you were a lovely note in songs played by buskers in the winter
You were all things bright and true
I gave you my best but it wasn't ever good enough for you
I was never enough for you

You taste like sweet honey on my lips
Or cocaine on fingertips
You sound like Holy words I knew
Sung out of tune
Or whispered soft in my bedroom
But you can't really whisper
I don't really mind
I've had tinnitus in these ears and your voice is so damned kind
I see you
In every perfect sunrise
I see me
A sad reflection in the brown of your eyes

NOT A FAN

She doesn't like you
She likes validation
Friendship without the obligation
She likes free dinner and something to do
She likes your company
But she doesn't like you

He doesn't love you
He loves the shape of your hips
Late night heavy breathing and consistent companionship
He loves the taste of your skin and the way you give him attitude
He loves netflix and chill
But he doesn't love you

SAME

I crave you still
In the quiet moments before bed
In traffic while visiting other cities
I want you during the exciting and mundane
But you,
You only wanted me when it was convenient
That's just not the same

APEROL SPRITZ AND OTHER POUR JOKES

1 1/4 oz Aperol
2 oz Prosecco
Splash of Soda water
This poem seemed funnier in my head
But I'm gonna publish it anyway

HIRAETH

It's in the mornings,
When sleep still grips tight to my conscious
It stays wrapped round my body
The way that you once were
As my eyes adjust from dreams to waking
As the sun warms the blankets we shared
It's during my lunchtime quiet
The sounds of chewing replacing your laughter
Soft, somber sips of water in the spaces we once spoke
And perhaps most resoundingly in evening
Light fading on a horizon that was more beautiful in your company
The absence of your conversation revealing a hollowness inside of me
I take walks
Past the church near my home and the park full of children practicing soccer
Next to the baseball fields
And of course
I miss you at the baseball fields
The truth is I never stopped missing you
The walk doesn't help like I hoped
And in the dead of night
I wake up
Silent home and empty bed
Looking for you
The parts of me hard to lose
A healing wound and persistent bruise
The girl I try to erase with distraction and booze
So I'll stop being so choosy
Bud light peeking out of a cheap foam koozy
Settle on some small town floozie
Hold on to her, but do it loosely
Sleep but only with two z's
Gotta admit I still miss you

LAST RITES

What if the last thing
you send me
is a fucking emoji

CHANGE

If I had known Denver was the last time I would kiss you
I would have done it better
I would have kissed you longer
Pushed you against the car
I would have grabbed your ass
I mean
I would have grabbed your ass *more*
I would have used tongue in a way that begs you to stay
Honestly
We should have been more naked
Even in that parking garage under your friend's place
I wish I'd left a better impression
And after all that
Both tangled in the passions of blind adoration
I wish I had told you I loved you
It might not have changed things
But if I'd known it was the last time
That's how I would change things

PERFECT DAY

Wild and lovely
Like flowers in a field sunkissed by the last light of a perfect day
A perfect day in which you accomplished your work
The things you set out to do
And spent time with friends in good company
Caught a game
And kissed a handsome older dude
In a sports bar in some city
God damn it
You've always been pretty
Wild, lovely, you
I think brown eyes are better than blue

APATHY STUFF

I hope that I never lose touch with the wonder of flight. Window seats on airplanes with the shutter pulled up and my face mere inches from the clouds and thin air of the heavens.
Flying into Hartford was one of the most beautiful things I've been able to experience in a life not terribly bereft of beauty.
My plane was taking off out of Maryland and it was probably 8 or 9 at night. The sun was completely set and the cities below were alight with street lamps and football fields and porch lights. The bloom and glow were surreal, and because the flight was shorter, the plane stayed at a much lower altitude, providing a closer view of it all. I stared out the window for almost the entire hour in awe of how the spider web of roads and haze of artificial light connected these disparate pieces of human life for miles and miles. I come from a state with almost infinite wilder-

ness. That may be why I'm so drawn to the bigger cities and industrial developments of the modern world. It's novel and lovely in a way that crop circles and flatlands stripped of greenery and trees have never been.

This felt like a science fiction film. Like Blade Runner. I was flying so close to some of humanity's weirdest and wildest achievements. Some of the roads seemed organic in the way that the wings of an insect are. Ordered but still alive. Unlike the grids of midwestern streets and regimented squares of small town development, the curves stretched and wound into and away from each other with artistic energy.

Or a structural need to avoid the environmental challenges of hills, and rivers and historical landmarks.

I prefer the former.

And that wonder, fifteen thousand feet in the air in a cramped Southwest Airlines 737, is something I want to hold onto. So much of the beauty we get to experience is tied to our ability to relax our brains enough to enjoy small things with big eyes and that's a thing I've struggled with for most of my life.

I'm cynical, depressed and angry. It's basically my twitter bio. I took a great deal of pride as a young guy in being willing to question anything, to remove the haze of misunderstandings explained as magical in favor of cold knowledge. Knowledge that would dismiss the magicians away. I'm working on that, but it's a substantial piece of my personality and I just loved the opportunity to stare out of that window, at almost 34 years old, feeling once more like a child without bills, and obligations and a never ceasing sadness that therapy cessates but never shakes.

For a little piece of a single evening, I felt as though the earth, this corner of it anyway, was kind of lovely.

I'm not alone. I think most people wrestle with melancholic misery and it can feel like a breath you never fully draw in, the panic of oxygen deficiency in a body incapable of ever reaching 100%. That's an analogy that doesn't read the room too well, so I may change it before publishing. Or maybe I'll leave it, I tend to awkwardly misread rooms anyway. It's authentic if nothing else.

I don't know where you're at. If you're reading this poetry book, I assume you've lived in that sadness or something like it at some point and I'm sorry. I hope that it gets better. But even in the shitty parts, I hope that you find your airplane window at night. Whatever that may be.

Maybe it's ice cream in a fresh bubble cone, or a friend playing music loud enough to leave your ears in a state of recovery for the week. Maybe it's just a hug from someone that cares for you. Whatever it may be, hold onto your wonder and remember it in the darker parts, of which there are so many. It can drive us to great things, so long as we navigate the emotional chaos with a touchstone of childhood novelty and wonder.

At least, that's what helps me. Streetlights from 15 thousand feet are a remarkable cure for apathy.

ACCOUNTANT

I keep a complex accounting
Of everything that I've done wrong
I play it on repeat in my head now
And it's in all my songs
Hey…
That's probably what's wrong

THE DREAM

I wanna talk about the weather in a bar that I don't like
Then hold your hair in silence while you turn your guts out and I
Claim this isn't what I wanted to be
But I just choose all the wrong people
And those people keep choosing me
I don't believe in god but I'm trying to change my tune
I sinned the day I told myself that I could fall in love with you

I'M LONELY

I'm lonely in ways constant and penetrating
Her eyes were too distant and her voice is grating
She lacked goals and ambition
Acting as though she was owed attrition
Like some goddess of the midwest
Some deity of the plains
I'm not enjoying dating
The girls here aren't my type
Or maybe I'm the problem
And that thought keeps me up at night
I'm lonely in ways I can't articulate
Ways I bury more with each shitty date

CIGARETTES AND SAINTS

I wish that I liked cigarettes
That aesthetic always seemed so cool
And when it's cold out
And I'm watching my breath turn to crystals and my knuckles shift to blue
I could be sucking carcinogens and charisma from inside of a paper tube
Pensive cold, cancerous breaths, under skies shifting in hue
All the miserable while,
Thinking about you

ALL GODS ARE THE SAME

All gods are angry gods
Just pick one to pray to
End your statements in prepositions
Nothing is sacred
Not all paths are clues
To the order the heavens arranged for us ants
As we juggle strange customs for some slight chance
At those pearly white gates
With pearly white teeth
I carry a pearl colored hatred inside of me
In the end it's all what we choose
Nothing here is sacred
Not even god
And definitely not you

OVER INVESTED

I'm always chasing heartbreak by over investing
In the under available
I try too hard to be clever and to remain unassailable
My logic is still fallible
My brain a chaos of useless paraphernalia
From the time we were together
Stitched into something I think will make us better
Resembling the leather jacket you wore on the day we first met
I bet
I could write a poem decent enough to keep you here
Something smart that causes the fog in our heads to clear
Sending us up past the clouds and the carbon emissions battered atmosphere
Into the heavens I knew were shaped for us
When I was a younger evangelical cosmonaut
But I'm not
That guy I was before
I'm just a dude form the internet that you don't like anymore

ARMCHAIREGGEDON

Grew up in a recession
Diagnosed with depression
Who isn't though these days?
It's looking like Armageddon
And where I've been heading
Has more to do with 90s cartoons
And silly PSAs
Than anything grounded in reality
I'm not angry enough at the elderly
That made the world this way

I'm too distracted trying to get laid

SETTLE DOWN

Anyone but you I'd be settling
Every step away from you is a step down
The high of your company followed by a come down
Hollow is a loud sound
Allow me to try and be profound
Actually don't read my shit
It isn't that great
It's just public catharsis after a few good dates

CAN'T C

Cadence and color change
Collectively conscious while creating clever concepts
Continuing to cull contemptuous coverage of your courage
Clearly correlated company copacetic to covalence in camaraderie
Cut concertedly
Along cartilage that's cornered and clean
Convoluted consternation cleaving creatively
As though at a christening,
You crystalline creature
Clearly covered in that coalescence of all creation
Claim that comforting compassion
Cling to the corruption
You captivating, compelling, courageous, coquettish, congenial fucking
Cunt

DAMN

I thought I would break my neck
The first day I saw you
Turning too fast not believing what I saw
You
Hair too perfect and a walk to match
See my twisting to stare might've caused that crack
Between the C1 and C2 vertebrae
I still struggle thinking of clever things I should say
To someone that has heard so many clever things
From men that probably have more hair than me
Men with pocketbooks larger than mine
And men with personality that doesn't rely
On self deprecation and television references
I'll ask if you have pronoun preferences
It's a conversational segway into something better I swear
I like the new colors that you've dyed into your hair
But there
Lies the problem with me
I'm distractible by all things colorful and pretty
And you
Are both colorful and pretty
No stunning
Maybe "resplendent" is better, see?
I can't even get these words to sound right
So I'll just get a neck brace and let your pretty face go
make someone else's night

YOU LIE PRETTY

She whispered that she loved me
I knew it wasn't true
I kinda like the lie though
It reminds me of you

NICKI MENAGE

Could I be your second husband?
Or if you've got a man I could be your third
But not in the bedroom
Just meant after you two
Figure out that you can't make it work
I've bought a couple rings by now
One more won't make or break me
But if you need a bad boyfriend
I have references that I'm a good kisser and
Remarkably mediocre company

LAKE LOVE

Love is the lake we both lead each other to
You were the water I never could see through
And at the bottom
Is where you'll find me
Still searching
Empty lungs craving oxygen
Sinking
Waiting
Dying
Inside of you

HOT GIRLS ON THE INTERNET

Just another hot girl on the internet
Someone clever I was lucky to have met
Netflix and countdown texts
My heart moved out of state and now I can't rest
Because of another hot girl from the internet

Derek Porterfield

STONES AND SHARP EDGES

It gets easier not because the road is less rough
But because your calluses grow thicker
Your eyes less wide
Your heart heavier
And the ground familiar
The stones and sharp edges cut all the same
We just grow more numb to that familiar feeling of pain

I AM BLISSFUL

There are those for whom the love and luster of life is buried beneath the burden of knowledge
It's a heavy weight, carried often alone
And for too brief a time, as it's burden so frequently leads to self conclusion

Not me though.
I'm dumb as hell.

Derek Porterfield

DOCTOR THUNDER

I don't go to doctors
I trust the universe
To kill me in whatever way she sees most fitting
Which is apparently clinical depression

Hahahahahahaha-
hahahahahahhaha-
hahahahahahaahahaha-
hahahahahahahahaha-
hahahahahahahahaha-
hahahahahahahhahaha-
haahahahahahahahaha-
hahahahahahhahahahaahahahahahahaha-
hahahahahahahahahahahahahahahahaha-
hahahahahahahhahahahaahahahahaahaha-
hahahahahhahahahaahahahahahahahahaha-
hahahahahahahahahahahahahhahahahaahaha-
hahahahahahahahahahahahahahaha

justkidding

READ THIS ONE DUMBASS

If they ever ask me to read my poetry on the news or something
I'll read this one
Not because it's particularly good
It isn't
Or because it's the shortest
It's not
But really how tall could a poem be?
It doesn't even rhyme
But won't that be kind of funny?
So on brand for me?
A chance to get new followers and I botch it
With even more bad poetry.

METH TOWN BOMB CITY HOMETOWN SO SHITTY

Meth addled Amarillo
Where underachievers stay and die
Where anyone of any consequence leaves to chase dreams and live life
The town from which there's no real escape
Where other failures promise that it's all okay
Things are getting better, they say
It's actually growing quite nice, right?
Two people got shot in drive bys last night
Have you seen me dude? I'm not good in a fight.
And it's not like that doesn't happen in Denver and Dallas too
But at least in those towns there's better things and prettier people to do
But when I buy my groceries
Or walk in the evenings I see cowboys
With eighth grade drop out diplomas and tobacco spit on their ceilings
How fucking bad does a city have to be
To make it something that causes its brightest to leave?
I hear what you're saying, dropping the eaves,
Nah that isn't the city that sucks, man
It's probably me

MEN WILL LITERALLY GO TO THERAPY

My therapist doesn't talk to me anymore
Thought his work was done and sent me out the door
That's how great I've shaped this emotional facade
Fuck therapy, I'll just take it up with God

QUIRKY

I'll make a quirky reference to a popular store or restaurant
Say a girl's name that sounds specific, but honestly it's not
I'll get your interest piqued with something relatable
Drive that engagement with something debatable
About the girls I chase
The ones I love
I'll make it sound funnier than it is because
I have crippling mental illness and it honestly kills me
To be earnest or share the ways that you don't fulfill me
So I'll talk about the playlist I made you
And joke about us fucking
Make a reference to Buffalo Bill and that scene where he's tucking
I'm not sorry
Just stating the ways
I try to appear as though I'm ok

THE STRANGULATION OF THE BISHOP

This poem is about masturbation
It isn't great
It's pretty quick
But it's honestly more for me

Derek Porterfield

COLORFUL

Nothing more American or trite
Than drinking an excess of reds and whites
To cure your living blues

PSL

Just ordered my first ever Pumpkin Spice Latte
I got the espresso blonde like a fall aerosol spray
Fitting, yes?
I sent my cousin a text
I feel basic and honestly don't know what's next
Should I get a hydro flask?
Stickers on the outside of my favorite brands
Listen to Taylor Swift Folklore in off white vans
Sell my house and drive my car around with no real plan
Should I buy an iPhone
A MacBook too?
And a watch to match the color of those off white shoes
Post pics on my insta of every single move
Because the value of my life is tied to the aesthetic of the things that I do
I just took a drink of a pumpkin spice latte
Sweet like the words I once used in her company
A white flag that I'm giving up on being hip or something
Existential dread over a god damned latte
Oh God
What the hell is wrong with me?
This is second wave
And I should prefer third wave coffee
Somebody, dear god, anybody please stop me.

Derek Porterfield

PRIORITY

The eyes rest before the body
The mind sleeps last of all
Priorities and solitude are a struggle for us all

RUDYARD KIPLING SHIT

If you can be spontaneous,
Exciting,
Rebellious with a little bit of edge
But be stable and caring and reliable,
All those, ALSO, not instead,
If you can make money
Enough for comfort and then more
Enough to buy whatever you want and make your children not so fucking poor
But don't focus on the money
It can't mean to much
If you can be relaxed and not always focus on work and the rush
If you can be great in bed but not sleep around
Be a virgin who still knows how to go down
If you can be this or that or whatever the shit
If I hear another rule I might fucking lose it
If you can't be everything and at the same time be nothing
They'll just leave you and go out to find their something

UNDONE

Undoing what is sacred
Making the precious feel cheap
I want to kiss enough people to make you feel less important to me
I want to wash the feel of your hands in mine away with the feeling of someone else's skin
I'll write wax sealed letters to strangers on the internet to seem as though I cared less than I did

DECEMBER BIRTHDAYS

Fart jokes are hilarious
Are you a sagittarius?
You seemed a bit nefarious
But I like that I don't have to carry this
Conversation
Your eyes dripping with elation
On the mundane shit
The crazy shit
The things we do together are the craziest
And the laziest
And I'm not sure who this lady is
But she makes me believe in love
And for this tiny moment in time that's enough
For the space of that breath I held in a city where you
carved new roads into creases in my mind
I felt it
And that's a wonderful, tiny bit of magic
Promise you felt it too
I get lost sometimes and invest my time
In people that are just being nice
I don't want to feel that way so don't answer
Just smile and say
I was whatever is the opposite of a bummer
An important part of your summer
And we can leave it at that

YOU SHOULD SIMILE MORE

A good simile is like
I don't know, honestly
But you are no simile
You are beyond compare
Nothing else like you exists for language to mangle beyond repair
You are sunrises and sunsets the eyes can't digest
More than beauty
More than love or lust or longing and yet,
You are the aching ever present in my chest
I could give my best to the universe that created you
And still fall short of the notion of deserving you
No,
You are unlike anything
You are all metaphors and no simile
You are the very best of the net sum of everything

NYQUIL

I'm still losing sleep over
Wishing I was under
You

UNHAPPY

I had way more luck with girls when I was
Selfish
Less kind
When I lacked in compassion
For the ones occupying my time
But
Again
I was unhappy then
Too

DAFT PUNK

They're playing that song we love and the bar is closing
Think I'll stay just a little bit longer
Cause that girl with a whiskey and coke she looks just like you
Think I'll drink until my courage is stronger
Cause you're still a Daft Punk melody
In my veins like methamphetamines
I can't stop buying what you're selling me
I need you to breathe
Next to me
Cause you're so lovely
Darling you're clever
You could do so much better
But I'm glad you're next to me

STAR TREK REFERENCE

You're the main character of your own story
That implies plot armor
Act like it
Be bold and move without the caution of secondary characters
Other people wear the red shirts while you topple barriers
With bare hands and a bare chest
Chiseled like the greek gods
Don't forget the pen you hold as you shape the lines that form your plot.

CHARON and KAREN

The guy that ferries boats across River Styx is named Charon
Pretty sure it sounds like "Karen"
In the present climate I find that kind of funny
I hope his mannerisms match the bob cut, dyed blonde women with money
In the Olive Garden screaming at the high school kid
I feel that attitude sits well on the river Styx
I think Charon and Karen would likely get along
Listening to all the same shitty Rascal Flatts songs
Floating a river and reveling in
The power they have over people lesser than them

DOWN DOWN BABY

You know those hand clapping games that girls play on the playground in elementary school?
The male equivalent, I assume, would be anything involving bodily harm in a group
Bloody knuckles
Slap boxing
Real boxing
But as a kid I was always fascinated by the speed and complexity of those sing-song clapping games that the girls played
Down down baby, down by the roller coaster, sweet sweet baby I don't wanna let you go
All while contorting their hands through a complex choreography of secret handshake worthy acrobatics.
Now that my daughter is in third grade, the mystery of this girlish society is being revealed to me.
Moreover, I'm being TAUGHT these games.
And I love it
And I suck at it.
She remembers the words and motions after what I have to assume is merely one recess of repetition whereas I struggle to remember the order in which I am supposed to clap or the correct number of hand flips before we switch up
It's great though
Being inducted into the secret society
Their handshake no longer a mystery
My daughter, so graciously including me
Down Down baby, down by the rollercoaster
My sweet sweet baby
I'm never gonna let you go

I Am Not In A Good Place
HOLDING HANDS

It is not for too much longer that my daughter will want to hold my hand
Tonight
We walked along sunset sidewalks talking about big things in small ways
Space travel and why it's so expensive
The kind of four wheeler we would purchase
if such an opportunity were to arise
The way you put on a t-shirt
Arms first?
Or head?
The girl she likes in her third grade class
The girl that she doesn't
The twin boys that play alone on the playground
Making friends
And why that's so hard
The sound hummingbirds make when flying
What she thinks the feral cats should be named
And it won't take long for her to stop sharing those things with me
To grow silent
To struggle with the horrible bits that humans discover as we age
To push me away while she tries to define her own life on her own terms
I hope that she knows she isn't alone
That I am a steady stone beneath her feet
A place in which she can find solace.
But for now, I will relegate those thoughts to an older man
For now,
I will walk with my daughter
And I will listen
And I will treasure every moment that she wants to hold my hand

DON'T FIGHT THIS FIRE

Years of stop drop and roll training
You learned in your elementary school
The firefighters preparing you for an uncertain future
All that rote memory
The practice drills
The challenge of children against a terrible fate
Was preparing you for when I finally drop my next mixtape

ADVICE

Advice for my daughter
Long walks cure short tempers, take them regularly
Specificity is the heart of apology,
Actions more and words sparingly
God is wherever you invest your spirit, make yours a kind one
Love is a language we learn over a lifetime, don't rush it's understanding, be willing to listen
Always choose short term over long term pain
Kindness is most important, in yourself and those you spend time with
Laughter is the best indicator of a healthy romance, pay attention to the people that make you smile
Listen with compassionate ears and speak love to everyone
Don't let humility get in the way of boldness and resolve, you have talents and they were earned by you, not given by any god
Be proud of yourself, but mindful to never cross the line to arrogance
You can ALWAYS learn more
You gain nothing by taking from others
You gain everything by sharing what you have
Above anything else learn to question
The world, it's leaders, your teachers, friends and yes
Please, never stop questioning me

NO CAP

The last girl that I dated wore baseball caps
I bought a baseball cap
I wanted to impress this girl
We watched baseball, I learned about baseball
Made sense with the cap
I wanted to impress this girl
She didn't live here so I traveled
A little back and forth
Cause I wanted to impress this girl
And I did
It worked
I kinda impressed this girl
We held hands and made plans
The intimate dance of two people life seems to like
We talked on facetime and shared fractional lifetimes
And I became myself insofar as someone can
When I was with this girl

DAUGHTER

My daughter doesn't know to be embarrassed by me
She's still young enough to embrace joy over apathy
It's remarkable how bright her eyes can be
We all once embraced that innocent love
Before the world melts us down into amorphous blobs
It's in our power
It's our charge and duty
To mold what is left into our own new kind of beauty

Derek Porterfield

RUPI WHO

My love for you (big)

I Am Not In A Good Place

Yours for me (small)

MOURNING COFFEE

In
The quiet chaos of mourning
That bitter taste of coffee and tears
My head and heart ache just the same
Even after all these years

BOYFRIEND MATERIALS

You're on your way to my place
To tell me more about his
And the life you'll someday live brick house and couple of kids
I kid
Sorta
You miss him even when I'm around
I don't have the personality to offset the distance and it's compounded by us

You were always going to be transient
Warned me right from the start
And I foolishly played along as though I could separate head from heart
You are smart
The med school variety
I try to make up for what I lack with charm and personality
You reminded me
Time and time again
You weren't staying long
Already had a good boyfriend
I sometimes wonder how good he could be
If he was okay with you staying with me
I honestly don't get the new trends in dating
I'll just float along thankful you gave me
A chance
Or moment
I guess

Lovely

You are lovely
The adverbial manifestation of love itself
"Ly" is an adverb, right?
The descriptive action
You are compassion
Kindness
Transcendent and striking beauty
It's your wit too
Sharp and biting
but kind
Always careful and comfortable
Mindful of me
You can't know what that means

I can't tell you that
Yours is a smile I find myself returning
even in your absence
You remain on my mind as a constant
Pleasant, ever present, and yes, lovely

I wanted to tell you how those sharp, intelligent eyes arrest my heart.
Even from the very start,
Above your n95
Those catchlights
Reflected back at mine
If I were ever as clever as you I'd rhyme
something with cardiomyopathy
To try and convey how broken my heart will be
With you gone

But I'm not that clever,

And I won't say goodbye

I'll just relish the alchemical wonder of your presence
That small bit of magic that comes from the company of someone so fascinating
The nervousness I still have when your hand brushes mine,
The soft kisses and subtle shifts of your body on the bed where we would lie
You and I
In the fading sunlight
But I won't say goodbye

I won't tell you
How difficult this is to navigate
Because however much I may struggle I know that you understate
Where you're at
You have it harder than me
I'm not blind to that
And I won't tell you how much I'll miss you cause that really isn't fair
But we have something, that feels important, sitting on the tension of unspoken words between us in the still air
I am
So eternally grateful for the fortuitous confluence
That allowed us to meet
However briefly
I don't want to see you go, selfish as that may be, but
I can still find beauty in the fractured pieces of experience
I got to share with you

I won't admit to how often I think of you
I won't tell you how much I've dreaded your absence.

I won't whisper in your ear, as I kiss lightly on your cheek, that
I love you
Even though I do
Even as all these things are true
I can't say any of it to you

So I'll pretend that I'm cool and agree here at the end
That yea,
You have a very lucky boyfriend.

Jeremy Bearimy

To my Eleanor Shellstrop,
In this hell and all that come after, I hope that I find you again.

This entire book

was made possible because of an incredibly loyal and supportive group of friends and strangers that supported my Kickstarter. See, on Kickstarter, if you don't make your goal dollar amount, everyone gets refunded and nothing happens. You only get to do the cool rewards and stuff if you hit your goal amount of funding. I launched that site with full understanding that I would likely have to fund it myself when it fell short just to make it work and yet…You guys blew past the goal and even hit the stretch numbers. I am so very rarely genuine, but I mean this from the depths of me: Thank you. I cannot believe this many people care about what I write and want to throw their hard earned money at my work. I am grateful. And I'm also apologetic. This took much longer than I anticipated. Particularly the custom poems. I was expecting to write maybe two or three but in the end there were FOURTEEN. I took my anxious time with the interviews and then really wrestled with how to write each of your poems. I wanted them to be funny, but also to relay the enormous amount of love I feel for you. Especially those of you that have known me since I was a god damned teenager. You've just helped to support the things that have shaped a large portion of my self identity and honestly, without that support, I don't know that I would have had the nerve to continue chasing these pieces of my heart that I love so much. The music, the books, and even my business, are all possible because of you guys and your humbling loyalty. You have shared me with strangers and bumped the tunes in your car and spread my bullshit videos on tiktok and socials and I just appreciate it. And you. So I hope you enjoy these poems I wrote for you. Your patience with this book is deserving of praise. Thank you for supporting me, and loving me, and helping me grow up by lifting me up. I probably love you.

And thanks for the money.

TARYN

She wanted to be an ice skater,
Like Michelle Kwan
Or maybe more accurately one of the russian ones,
But when I met Taryn we were pretty far from the USSR
Listening to the kind of shitty music teenagers cry to in their cars
She was cute with a smile that seemed to never leave her face
And I really only saw her in one particular place
The hospital on sixth
Trying it's best to fix
The wayward, strange and outcast kids:
The motherfucking 806.
And it's strange now
To look back on a girl I didn't know all that well
She's a mother
Scrappy, strong
Proud of the pieces of life she has overcome
And it's impressive
As a guy who grew up self defined by my depression
To see someone achieve as much as she has
Cause as kids this wasn't a future I'd ever imagined
I can't speak for her but I don't know what happened
I blinked a few times
And suddenly life
Became something completely foreign and new
And that happened to her too.
I'm lucky for the people I met singing shitty songs
In a misfit haven disguised as a coffee shop
But Taryn is one I feel lucky to still call friend
So for Taryn
I hope she puts on those skates
And continues to chase

I Am Not In A Good Place

The dreams of that younger woman
while raising one of her own
It's the best part of life to become the person
You knew you could be all along.

MACHELLE

The voice of an angel was dressed as a demon on Halloween night last year
Her horns peeking out from a head full of artistry and creativity -
My vision clouded only slightly by the beer
And the demon sang with me,
Elegant harmonies
Her wings seemed to spread and flex their strength
And from perhaps my favorite stage
I shared a song in a strangely perfect place
With her,
As though rising from hell
We all watched Machelle
Steal that stage
And it was lovely
The night was not saccharine, but sweet
And now,
A magical wonderland of escapist fever dreams
A place made of unbridled talent and psychedelic retreat
This demon has made something wild and wonderful and crazy
An art space of exploratory paradoxical visual expression
And in this magical space,
If you look closely,
You can probably find a small piece
Of the demon that once sang with me

THEATER WEIRD

On an Irish shore
Fresh tea on the kettle
Fireplace lit in a sweet cottage ripped straight from the pages of Tolkien
A curious girl might be making jewelry
Or painting something lovely
Or smiling lightly at the neighbors while jamming songs from David Bowie
"Curious" seems to short sell her
It's a word not quite worthy
Hers is a anomalous sort of character
A strangeness in it's unwavering honesty and brightness
I mean
She's had her art sent to the moon
The tidal-locked entity brightening our darkest skies
How appropriate
How nice a place for her art to lie
And if you were to travel to the moon
Maybe get Elon Musk or some other eccentric billionaire to take you
You might catch her pre-raphaelite artistry
Near aliens admiring the brushwork on now-dry uncharted seas
She is unique
Bravely sidestepping any fears
My friend Adrian is the coolest sort of
Theater weird

ANDREW MONROE

Andrew Monroe is the reason I write at all
Not in the same way that my many exes have inspired
weeping words on tear-stained pages
Not quite
But
He showed me it was possible
To write something and share it with the world
And to be fair he probably did it better than me
Certainly with much more courage than me
And with a great deal more maturity
But still
After him
Was me
And it really didn't start with the books
He drug me to the gym to help compensate for my bad looks
And reportedly "difficult" personality
Convinced me we both might one day be vikings
At a time in my life where I was abandoned by everyone,
He kept my feet beneath me
Brought me too much caffeine
He made me stronger despite my burgeoning apathy
So for everything I have done since
Blame Andrew, not me.
Then Andrew met Shalomi
His once calloused exterior
that mirrored
My own
Softened and he seemed to grow
Just ever so much happier
She drew out a softness uncommon in my cousin
And it was crazy to watch him become the little bitch for once
Finally I could be the one

Making fun
Of him
But it didn't phase him of course
Barbs hurt less with a pretty girl on your arm
A girl he somehow captured despite his almost total absence of charm
She kept him smiling more than he had in years
More than after he's had 6 or 7 beers
He gives her coffee and Target on Saturday
and she gives him the sort of company that can offset even his darkest malaise
Sounds like a decent trade
To me
So thanks Andrew,
I'm glad you found Shalomi and got your life somewhat sorted
And hope that you finally feel supported
But most of all
I'm glad you were never aborted
Despite your unfortunate face that apparently more than a mother learned to love.

CHRISTIAN

Do you know the Muffin Men?
The Muffin Men
How in the hell do I write about one of the original Muffin Men?
We were a group of middle school kids with almost enough rebellion between us to spit in a hallway
Just enough edge to cut warm butter in a desert
Almost as dangerous as a strong wind in early spring
I was proud to be among them
Christian was arguably the coolest of our group
Which, is not staggeringly impressive
But still worth noting
He had swag before I knew what swag was
He cared less but still excelled and had way more luck with the ladies
He even walked cooler
Which was important to me in middle school
Anyway
The Muffin Men (The muffin Men)
Would go chalk houses
Toilet papering was a bridge too far
In the wee hours of the night-
Our jolly group of boys cosplaying as men would sneak
Into a van driven by a consenting adult
And find friends needing a good artistic addition to their driveways
Basically a modern Jesse James, each and every one of us
Now
Christian is older
And much to my chagrin
He is even cooler
Married to a girl named Shelby
Conversation so engrossing they forgot about their coffee

She is a kindness in his life, a giver, and full of patience and gentleness
A necessary characteristic when married to Christian
It's a wonderfully sweet romance of shared passion and love
And now
Six years on,
Shelby gave him Amelia, their beautiful daughter
Changing my friend the Muffin Man
Into a full blown Muffin Father

MORGAN

Morgan is perhaps my most abused cousin
"The family whipping post" could be a name tag on her purse
We have probably called her worse
Her decision making is so poor it begs for change on street corners in badly lit parts of town
Her taste in romance eschews fine dining in favor of dumpster diving in an evening gown
She craves chaos and story over everything
Which is why I get along with her so well I think
She is an awful lot like me
I mean that insultingly
Give her a suggestion and she will do the opposite
I compete with her regularly on who can talk more shit
She picks fights consistently. Fights she knows she won't win
Just for the turmoil in the family tree's soil
She stirs the pot before absconding again
And Amarillo is so much worse for her absence
The gossip I craved is missing and from habit
I sometimes look around when someone says something stupid or erratic
Or a family member brings up something problematic
And Morgan isn't there
To share in the embarrassed glee
Or to fight the fam
Against or with me
So to my Houston cousin
My favorite to offend
And the one I miss most when thanksgiving ends:
Date better dudes
You deserve brighter people
You're too cool, clever, and pretty for men so

I Am Not In A Good Place

Fetal fecal feeble
Just fools wasting your time
Quit hanging with 3s when you know you're a dime
I won't name any names cause that's not polite
But seriously dude, you know that I'm right
And if I'm not come back to rillo and fight me about it
I need someone here that's better at talking shit
Miss you
And all the opportunities I no longer have to diss you.

CARTER

Giggly, shy Carter
Full of sweetness – so kind
Her heart is a reflection of her mother's love
And that reflection is beautifully bright
Like her eyes
On an adventure in some created world
Carter understands that the strongest among us have always been the girls

Hers is an adventure club
They even have a cool rhyme
"Brave and strong and smart and kind
we are the adventurists all the time"
And time is something less fleeting
When your eyes are as wide as hers
It's a lovely, beautiful freedom for which your whole childhood is worth

And maybe Carter is on a scooter,
Heading to the coi pond with dad
Or maybe she is playing make believe
On a trampoline
Regardless, she does both of them fast
Cause this girl does everything quickly
In a rush before she's beckoned to bed
Kissed lovingly and with covers pulled to just below her little red head.

Carter is a joy everyone can feel
I hope she holds onto that tight
Cause the world needs more girls like Carter
A brightness in a world without light.

I Am Not In A Good Place
JANSEN

There is a girl named Jansen
Who loves to draw and paint
Her work is a modern marvel
Line work could be mistaken for that of a saint
Cause saints draw really well
Trust me
It's a thing
Don't look it up
If the next generation is lucky
Though so few really are
She will become a teacher and share
The craft and care
That goes into creating her art
And in some ways that art is shaped by her mother
Always so kind and nice
Praising the work and loving her fiercely
All while sharing that token mom-type advice
Like "fold that this way"
Or "Just let the dogs play"
Or "Please eat your veggies and rice"
I don't know how she says it
These are just guesses
But I assume I'm at least partially right
So Jansen I'll need
A drawing or some-thing
To point to in a decade or two
To tell both my friends
I knew you back when
You weren't famous, just precocious and cool
Seriously,
I want to buy a drawing.
For real

HADLEE

Hadlee was the girl with the hardest job
The daughter that had to be first
The first for mom is the first for her
And the first is sometimes the worst
Cause there's so much to learn, for you and for her
And the struggle is shared like a curse
But on the other side of that early struggle are the memories of making things work
Of baking stale bread into crackers
And laughter on Saturday nights
Of art studios
And Coraline prose
And a mom that would always make time
Time that moves quickly
Much too quickly
As two girls stubble along
One a young woman
The other a child who made that young woman a mom
And now with two siblings
Hadlee keeps listening
And growing
And sharing
Alot
Cause the girl that takes the first step
Is the bravest
I say this
As the best thing I may have ever been taught
The path you blaze is difficult
specifically so
That someone else's path is not
Be proud of the life you've lived
And keep loving on both the other two kids
And if it ever feels like too much to shoulder
Remember us first borns are coolest
Simply because we are older

TALON

There's a man that boxes Kangabros
Skydives naked
Like seriously. NO clothes
Just flopping around out there
Slapping and clapping in the wide open air
He met a pretty girl and lost her for six long years
Then he saw her again and less than a week later got married, now they have kids
He isn't just a paragon of manliness and charm,
His sharp gaze and chiseled body sets off fire alarms,
He is more than the sum of his objectively perfect parts
My man Talon also has a beautiful heart
A friend that I've had for over 15 years
Who supported me loudly while I cried my emo boy tears
This dude is Morgan Freeman from Bruce Almighty
Basically god, I don't say that lightly
He saved a kid that was missing his limbs while on deployment
I can't imagine a more difficult brand of employment
But this mythical beast of a man shrugs off death and praise in the same casual way
That must be what was attractive to his (now wife) Stephanie
Entranced by the man who hangs brain while skydiving
The dude that could do literally anything
With the girl willing to jump at those same opportunities
They have the sort of crazy love only storybooks can talk about
A romcom without a credits scene
They're just living it all out
And they made incredible kids from whom we can expect a great deal
But if we are being less subtle, more blatantly real
The man has one fault I haven't yet mentioned

Something that gains a bit of internet attention
You see,
Talon can never resist the siren call of
An unlimited, lifetime supply of olives.
So if you see this superhuman beast on the street
Gift him a small potted olive tree
Or maybe a can of Thassos from Greece
Or Kalamata to chew with those perfect smiling teeth
As long as it's olives this man will be happy
And that keeps him up in our skies still flapping.
We love you Talon, not to be too sappy,
But next time you skydive feel free to wear some khakis

MIMI & PAWPAW

Grandparents have such an interesting role
Love unconditional
But like tenfold
Compounded by each generational jump
They have the kind of love that takes on way too much
The kind that says "yes" when it should have been no
Stay up late
Ruin your clothes
Eat this quick before you go home
It's the type of love that transcends our parents
One that's less Cameron and a little more Ferris
From a wiser perch they can see how big things aren't quite so big as all that
And that it's true, life moves pretty fast
See,
They can listen better, despite the hearing aids
They have the fancier, cooler brand of band aids
But more than anything else
And perhaps best of all
My own grandparents filled in gaps while playing three roles
From Parent to Grand and from Grand to Great
They earn that last word with every Hazel Mae play date
They wake up early and stay up too late
With a gentle sort of kindness while watching her play
And explore and learn and grow
In the safest and most comfortable place I've called home
Grandparents play an interesting role
And mine have consistently warmed my whole soul

TYLER & BETHANY

Tyler is like my brother, but that sounds bad
I would never insult him by implying we had the same bio-dad
But ever since that fateful vacation
In the most sinful of American tourist locations
After a handful of reasonably strong libations
I told him he could be a little more patient
I told him
 "Wait to marry my cousin
You've got time and there's no sense in rushin"
(He didn't, Thank god,
I have a very cool, very marry-able cousin)
Ever since then he's been family
Feels kinda like we are Turk and JD
But the kind of Turk that I never get to see
Because see, Turk was stolen from me
By that marry-able cousin, Bethany
She whisked him away and hid him from our crew
In a much bigger city with a lot of cooler things to do
She forced him out of the plains and into somewhere with trees
Around people who passed more than just elementary
A place where they both work fantastic jobs
and spend time with each other whenever they're off
Away from the drama of family and politics
They created a space that keeps relationships from getting sick
But shit
I'm sick
Cause I miss Tyler
(Bethany too I guess)
I wish he could 3D print me something to fill this hole in my chest

I Am Not In A Good Place

But it's for the best
Cause they have this sort of love that is rare in my family
See, when I hold hands I do it clammily
But they got this figured out and when we
Finally see them around the Christmas Tree
They seem happier than us
Like they have a relationship built on trust
Like they don't shit on each other, they just build each other up
Board games and cookouts and cocktails and reading
They're the type of people everyone should try being
But you won't be able to
Even if you try
Cause Bethany is too smart
And Tyler is just too cool of a guy
So I'll have to settle on misery
Absent of Tyler (and Bethany's) company
And now more than ever, in this nearness hiatus
I'm glad Tyler ignored my ass when we first talked in Vegas

RACHAEL

A beautiful sonographer at Texas Tech
Hired a stranger on the internet
And I honestly don't get
Why the hell you would let
A weird guy like me take your money
I mean thank you,
I hope that you think that I'm funny
But like
Think of all the other things you could buy
This was around Christmas time
So you coulda had some cutco knives
Or like an ugly festive sweater
I mean thank you
Don't worry, this poem gets better

See Rachael was a teen mom
Before it was trendy and chic
Before MTV would follow you around for a week
And exploit your struggle for views and try to seek
The approval of other young teens
Nah
Rachael did it all with just a fistful of grit
A highschool girl with a kid on her hip
And a stiff upper lip
And a distinct absence of television crews
She simply did what she had to do
It's true
She's much cooler than me and you.

And at 15 years old
She would meet a cute guy
He was on another date but thought Rachael was nice
He was right,

(Don't let your girlfriend keep you from finding your wife)
Sound advice
Cause now they've been married for TWENTY FIVE Years
With two boys and the type of bond formed only in blood, sweat and tears
The kind of love that endures despite struggle and fear
The kind of love I cry about after too many beers
It's admirable and remarkable and after all this time they're still here
And the dude chose right
Rachael is a fantastic wife
The kind of girl that makes burdens feel light
That elevates them both to entirely new heights
And that's just a beautiful thing
So, good job dude on getting that ring
And thank you Rachael for trusting me
Hope the words I'm writing leave your eyes feeling starry
And if you don't like it
I guess, thank you
I'm sorry

TEYSHA & MATT

Not to brag
But I'm the greatest wingman that has ever existed
The absolute best "getting laid assistant"
I have quite a few half-decent references
But I gotta say that the best of them is
Definitely Matt and Teysha
Matt has been a best friend and therapist
A patient teacher with unmatched rizz
That's a word I stole from tiktok kids
He's cool. That's what I mean
He's a badass with class and a brain that can not only pass but run circles around me
I've slept in this man's spare bedroom during a breakup
He's taught me how to repair dents and replace brakes on his pick up
He's a guy that's survived despite wildly oscillating luck
And I'm not saying I could ever repay him
I can't. No way in fuck.
But I setup his Bumble
I took all his photos
And he met the absolute perfect woman soooo…
Like, he didn't walk into her, my man just stumbled
Then almost immediately after, he damn near fumbled
See it was a twist of fate
Matt figured Teysha was fake
Which, from his perspective, lowered the stakes
A bit
But this man is an absolute idiot
I mean that respectfully
But after he went camping he
Completely ghosted this angel from the world wide web
Cause he has something seriously wrong in his head
But Teysha saw something special

Probably because the profile I made him was on a whole nother level
Regardless, this woman's patience is matched only by her smile
And despite this man choking harder than someone rapping against Jimmy Smith Jr in 8 mile,
She hit him up once again
My man took her to Fuzzy's
He doesn't even kiss her does he?
Side hugged her like a dummy
And she's still here.
Matt's lucky
Been like 3, maybe 4 years?
Too many seasons of Chicago Fire and PD
They both share the same favorite memory,
I won't put it here, I promised, but it's sweet.
I think even separately they speak volumes of love
It's in the way that Teysha's name makes his face light up
Or the soft smile she gives him when he's grilling steaks that he stuffed
In a relationship defined and shaped by Dick Wolf's perfect screenplays
Theirs is a love everyone hopes that they find someday
A shared resolve to put in the work
A safe space for Matt to learn to twerk
She speaks of my best friend in a way that is truly, deeply, humbling
And my man Matt is a lucky man for her company
And he knows it
This type of thing is found so very seldom
So to both Matt and Teysha:
Yea yea,
You're welcome

ANDREW BRANDT

There are few worse people than Andrew fucking Brandt
Ugly to the point of being difficult to look at
And you might think he offsets it with charm or personality
But no
He lacks both of those and still lives life so damned casually
We've insulted each other in our book's acknowledgements pages
Jabs that will live past us both for the ages
You can read about his lack of redeemable qualities
Or his perception of my attempts to sound as wise as Socrates
But I'm an anomaly
He's the US economy
Shambles and a shell of his former self
But when I finally meet him again down in hell

I might admit he's been a pretty cool father
And he has a wonderful wife and he knows he's lucky to have caught her
Most of us speculate he had to have bought her
But it's not true,
She actually digs this dude.
And even though I wrote this fully intending to be rude
I have to balance it out so I don't get sued
He's got a talent for authorship
Prolific and established as shit
And his work is enjoyed by much more than just me
So Andrew please see
I love insulting you buddy
But I love it the most
That this insult cost you money

The Bad Place

Over the last few years I wrote a handful of essays and a collection of random thoughts to offset the soul-crippling boredom that was 2020-2021. I liked doing it and would love to carve out the time for it again. It was more of a public journal than anything else but, what better to fill the pages of a poetry book than the earnest musings of a depressed dude in lock down? The following are some of those essays and I hope you dig em. This first one is actually my favorite.

UNREQUITED

Do you know what the most common form of love is?
You might guess, platonic, or romantic. Or if you've been reading the five love languages, maybe you'd assume physical love, or gift giving, or quality time.
The truth is a simple sadness: The most common love is unrequited.
I know, it sounds as though my inner emo is coming out, but I actually think this is kind of beautiful.
You meet a girl, right? She's pretty and funny and when she talks, about anything really, the world seems to go in slow motion. You notice the way light refracts differently through her hair in the sunset, and that she smells good. Like really good. You go on dates and talk about life and goals and everything magical and mundane in breathless adoration for each other.
It's great right?
The feeling you get in your stomach when the universe is

clicking into place, just for you, is one of the most profound and intrinsically human experiences available to us. I think that its rarity is perhaps the coolest part.

More often, we see the girl, and try to match eyes. She waves and we wave back to the horrifying realization that her greeting was intended for the friend behind you. Or perhaps you found a guy that you really dig, and manage to get that date. Maybe several. You find a rhythm, which isn't easy to do and in that awkward dance of dinners and bowling and cute walks in the evening, you believe sincerely that you've found someone. But he doesn't feel that same energy. You're nice and all, but it's just not working. You say "tomato" he says "I'd like to see other people". Or whatever.

If not for those moments, that feeling of elation followed so closely by its kissing cousin of devastation, we would be so much less capable of appreciating the magnitude and wonder of mutual affection.

When someone sees beyond your instagram painted visage and somehow manages to connect with your soul, when they see the ugly and the plain, and the honest, open truth of you and don't look away, that's as close as we really get to heaven down here.

There's a quote, perhaps my favorite, from Rothfuss in The Wise Man's fear. He says:

"In many ways, unwise love is the truest love. Anyone can love a thing because. That's as easy as putting a penny in your pocket. But to love something despite. To know the flaws and love them too. That is rare and pure and perfect."

I film love and its many wonderful promises for a living. I was asked recently if it was difficult to work weddings while struggling to date in my own personal life, and…. no, but also….more honestly, yes. Absolutely.

I mean, I don't think about it alot, but there's a different kind of loneliness that strikes when editing a love story of a beautiful couple while drinking whiskey in an empty house, with the sounds of a computer fan and clicking keyboard providing the only company.

It's that sadness, or perhaps more accurately, that hollowness, that makes discovering the right person so much more profound. When the resounding echoes of your life find a place in which they can finally be still. The comfort and joy we realize in another person that, through no small twists of fate, returns your attraction, is a remarkably rare and wonderful feeling.

To be honest, my point in all of this has very little to do with love. I'm certainly in no position to offer advice on that front anyway. Rather, I think I want to slow down and appreciate the less beautiful and unromantic pieces of living.

I'm not directing this movie. And though it pains me to admit it, I'm not the star in anyone else's film but mine. So to ignore or begrudge the parts that aren't fun and cute and filling my insides with butterflies is to disregard the broader strokes of the story. Things are tough for everyone right now, maybe the best response is to sit with that feeling a little while. Understand it.

The absence of anything makes its discovery all the more important.

Just like love, life is full of unreturned energy.

Until it isn't.

I hope you weather the storm and I hope you find a heart that matches your own. Cause you're a badass, and I probably love you.

THIRTY-THREE

When I was 12, a 33 year old wasn't just an adult, they were wise. As a guy that is now as old as the mortal Jesus, I realized that maybe I've always been kind of dumb. I've thought alot about this particular birthday. The religious subtext only accounting for a tiny fraction of those thoughts. I really wanted to be further along by now. I think that when I was younger I just assumed I would have found a higher level of success. Like, shouldn't I have a jet ski by now? I was under the impression that I would. That's not to say I'm ungrateful. I recognize and appreciate the enormous privilege of the life I'm living. I have, objectively, the best child on the planet who is constantly teaching me as I stumble through my own flailing attempts at doing the same for her. I work for myself and drink enough coffee to cause some pretty serious heart issues in a few years.
Yesterday, I didn't shower until 1 pm.

I am, by any measure, pretty damn lucky.
But that's the thing with luck. We all have this desire to earn something. To chase a goal and achieve it, but I think the irony is that we tend to shift the goal posts. No matter where you started, by the time you reach that first milestone you've learned enough to realize how shortsighted your initial ideas of success or achievement were.
I've been thinking alot about the music. I wanted a band that played a few shows and got to travel. Then I found out that it really doesn't require much more than just calling and asking to play somewhere to get a show booked in another city. So then I wanted to get paid. Which is also remarkably more common outside of my hometown. I traveled and got paid to play music and still felt as though I hadn't done much, because in reality, I hadn't. I was a kid with a guitar, asking adults if they would pay me to poorly cover Matchbox 20 in their coffee shops.
AND THEY DID.
Kind souls, each and every one.
The same goes for most of the tentpoles in my life. Chasing that elusive mistress we call happiness resulted in a lot of cool things, but never a true sense of accomplishment, and certainly not happiness.
So I started writing books. My cousin wrote a fantasy epic and caused me to reflect on the countless novels I had started in Google Drive over the years and never finished. No-Mod felt cool the entire time I was writing. It took a lot of work, but guess what? I was still unsatisfied. I wrote the next one, immediately throwing myself back into the project. It came out today. I don't care if you buy it. I'll sales-pitch it or something with another blog.
The meandering point is this: I've spent an entire life chasing the approval of other people and that will forever be a hollow goal of vapid motivation. My favorite quote

from the Showtime series "Californication" comes from Meredith to Hank Moody before she leaves: "You love women, but you hate yourself, so that any woman who ultimately does like you is deemed a fool."
It's a rephrasing of a common trope, "love yourself before anyone else can", but it's stuck with me for a long time.
I want my 33rd year to be one in which I am kinder to myself, and I hope writing this out maybe allows someone else to recognize their own self-admonishment as a negative trend and they join me in trying to be more chill.
Jesus died at 33 so maybe it's time I stopped playing the role of the martyr and started living life. Thanks for reading, I probably love you.

FATHER'S DAY

I'm lucky.
Extraordinarily so.
I'm a dad.
I have a daughter who still thinks I'm cool despite overwhelming evidence to the contrary. She still asks me questions, instead of google, because she believes in her heart that I'm a better option than the computer speaker in her room. She likes the music I show her, trusts me to choose movies and generally makes me feel like a much cooler version of myself.
She's remarkable. And thankfully not yet embarrassed by her old man.
Today she made me breakfast in bed.
I'm lucky.
"Our fathers were our models for God. If our fathers bailed, what does that tell you about God?"
That's a line from one of my favorite books/movies, Fight

Club.

It's true.

Before our kids are able to stumble through their own rough conceptualizations of spirituality and an afterlife, they are given us: flawed, under-educated children, masquerading in adult body suits, as their first deity.

And the importance of that parental role cannot be overstated.

I say "parental" role. It may be "father's day" but that has NEVER meant your biological sperm donor.

Maybe your bio dad was great! Good. Embrace that gift. But if he wasn't, that's okay too.

Maybe your mom raised you by herself and did her best to fill in the empty spaces. If you're able to read this, she prolly did alright. Wish her a happy father's day.

Maybe your dad sucks. An uncle, or grandfather or friend filled that role. That's good. And that's worth celebrating. Happy father's day to them too.

Maybe you can't think of anyone that close in your life. Maybe instead, it was a teacher, a coach, or a boss at a highschool job somewhere. Celebrate those wonderful people.

Today is about those formative models for God. That impossible role, that with hindsight, you can empathetically appreciate.

There's a scene in Guardians of the Galaxy 2 (*SPOILER ALERT*) where Yondu has just saved Star Lord (which is weird to type out, but hang with me) and this man is flying Star Lord into the sky. Yondu raised Star Lord in the absence of his own dad and honestly did a horrible job most of the time. But he really did try, he made an effort. An effort that Star Lord's father never did. Yondu says, in reference to Star Lord's biological dad, "He may have been your father, boy, but he wasn't your daddy." (*END

SPOILER*)

I hope that anyone out there who struggles this time of year can pause and remember someone that may not have been your father, but still filled the role of "dad".

Don't let societal expectations of fatherhood change the way you celebrate this holiday. Be thankful for the people in your life that were "daddy".

Or put a way that involves less snickering on the internet: Our fathers were our models for God. Celebrate the good ones.

Happy Father's day.

WALK

When I was in college, my best friend and I would walk from his apartment to the coffee shops or bars, often amounting to four or five hours of just walking and talking together. Whether this careless existence was more of impoverished necessity or for enjoyment I can't really remember, but it was a unique sort of calm before life begins to bludgeon you more thoroughly with responsibility. A time in my life during which everything still felt inspired and artistic.
And that wasn't just the alcohol.
Magical things happen when we walk. When we slow down enough to breathe in the smaller pieces of life's chaos. I remember playing music on a rooftop at 2 in the morning with complete strangers dancing along to the songs. I remember an abandoned building that was partially destroyed and screamed stories of an unseen apocalypse. We even broke into a construction site and

climbed a scaffold just to sit at the top and drink Shiner while feeling like complete and total badasses.

I wanted to recapture that. At least in part. See, the adventure doesn't need to be on the fringes of legality to release those euphoric friends we affectionately refer to as endorphins. Rather, I just wanted to take time away from the work I've been doing seven days a week for the last two years and find a state of moving meditation.

I know someone more educated than me is screaming at their screen that movement is antithetical to proper meditation but I kind of like that imagery. An angry monk. A monk that's angry at me.

So I found a few audiobooks and podcasts and donned my headphones for a dipping of my proverbial and literal toes into the purposeful act of not working. I started small. Maybe thirty minutes around the neighborhood. And when I came back home I returned to the computer and kept working.

And that doesn't really count.

I think the key is getting beyond that one hour mark. Chasing the point that you've legitimately interfered with time you could be making money and made a deliberate choice to do the opposite.

I decided to listen to a few episodes of this American Life and just walk until it got dark. The air was getting cooler and the light always seemed to look different in the fall and winter, so for the first half of the walk I was just appreciating that golden halo around all of the mundane parts of my neighborhood and enjoying my podcast. Even the trash cans seemed ripped from a Thomas Kinkade painting.

But it was around the first hour mark that I began to really pay attention to the things around me. The hidden throughway that was too small for a car that connected two cul de sacs near my home, or the basketball goal that was setup behind a fence with its net hanging into the paved alley for the kids to play on something more analogous to a court.

I saw trees that smelled like my first girlfriend's perfume (Velocity by Mary Kay). I saw children acting out bloody battles with swords and bikes and nerf guns.

More importantly, I saw myself. The overworked and emotionally barren husk that remained in the wake of a twenty something that actually believed that the world was beautiful.

That's a thing that I used to think about. The beauty in forgotten places.

I continued to walk and listen to some pretty remarkable stories on the podcast. There's a big park near my home and I decided to make a loop around it. I watched all the families that brought their kids to the playground and the dads that were teaching a few young girls soccer fundamentals. And at about mile 3 I forgot about the work I had left to do and the bills, and the upcoming meetings and the girl I was flirting with.

Okay, I was still thinking about the girl, but I mostly forgot the "adult" stuff and was able to feel the edges of calm for the first time in a while.

The walk home was euphoric and I found myself turning off the podcast and just walking in silence for a while, trying to breathe in the first whispers of fall and hold onto that fleeting brush with whatever the opposite of depression is called.

So I'm walking more. Chasing the dragon, as it were. That first high from when I was eighteen with a book of poetry and a desire to find the beautiful among the trash of my home town. And it's working, kinda. So if you've been down, and I mean, haven't we all been this year? I hope you take a walk, a long one, one that takes a dedicated and not insubstantial amount of your evening away just so you can see the sunset in the places you normally only glimpse while driving 35 mph in a 30 to get to the next appointment or obligation or whatever.

And if you really dig it, I hope you find a construction site and bring a few beers and watch the world from a new perspective for a bit. We're here too brief a time to negate the little things.

EMERGENCY

I've always found emergency contact forms to be a unique sort of aggressive.
Who cares about you? You know, when you die. Who will give a shit? That's what they're asking.
In addition to releasing whoever (or is it whomever?) from liability on the next page, they really drill home how few people you may have in your corner.
I mean, that's how it feels to me anyway.
When filling these out, I tend to vacillate between my uncle and whatever girl I may be dating at the time and both of those options, when written down, bring into focus something I never really talk about.
For reasons I won't be diving into, I don't speak with the immediate biologicals at all.
I want to be super clear: this is not a bad thing, nor do I hate the people that I grew up around.
If you happen to live a life of the more estranged variety

I assure you, that you are not weird or wrong and, insofar as you are making choices in a way that positively impacts your life, you are doing the right thing.

And that's why I'm hung up on these contact forms. In the place where so many people put down their mom or dad, some of us have the gift of writing down the family that we chose. And really, the family that chose us. An adoption without the paperwork.

When I was 15 years old I remember being upset. The reason doesn't matter. I headed to my aunt and uncle's home and they made coffee at an hour that any reasonable adult would avoid caffeine, and they stayed up late and talked to me and supported me. In many ways, this night was the catalyst that led to my relationship with this part of my family growing stronger. I could trust them and they treated me with a sense of respect that I think every adolescent craves.

Hell, adults too.

I worked for my uncle for years and that sense of mutual respect grew over the course of several arguments that lasted, I'm not exaggerating, literal weeks, about everything from politics to music. Around this time, he became the first change in my emergency contact. The guy I figured would be least likely to answer the phone but most likely to care if I died or became horribly mangled in some fashion.

There was also my bandmate, Trey. I've written a lot about him, but suffice to say he was the most profound friendship over the course of my childhood. He started the band, introduced me to Fight Club, which I probably talk about too much, and fostered a love of reading and a deeper compassion than my protestant upbringing had previously encouraged.

I could write a book about all the things I learned from

Trey. He was a really important person in my life. So he became the second big change to that form.
And that's why those are the only two phone numbers that I have memorized at 33.
There were some sporadic points at which my girlfriend's name would fill the space below the medical release and above the insurance information, but really, that was a kind of blind optimism, right?
Anyone with a passing knowledge of my music knows the girls don't tend to stick around very long and really, what would they do in the event of an emergency?
The idea of that phone call makes me smile.
"Yes, this is Derek's girlfriend, Haley Williams. Yes, the one from the multi-platinum selling band. What's wrong?"
"We're sorry but Derek is super dead."
"Oh damn. Well that's a bummer."
"Totally a bummer. So look there's these bills and funeral stuff..."
(The sort of heavy silence only a hospital can hold)
"We really only texted a few times..."
"We'll call the state to pick him up. Listen, Misery Business is a bop."
"Thank you so much!"
Or something like that.
And that's the power of that blank space on the emergency forms. Those people, often unbeknownst to them, are signed up for a different kind of hell should the information ever need to be utilized.
Death is a difficult thing in any circumstance but when you are the one tasked with navigating the specifics and the arrangements and the money, it is a uniquely persistent hell.
The ones doing that for you, in the absence of you, are of a particular brand of importance. The family that, in my case at least, runs deeper than blood.

So if you struggle with that space on the medical release, you aren't alone. I hope that you have someone you consider your chosen family. They really are the best. And if you don't' have that yet, feel free to write me down. When Haley Williams texts me back, our family would be happy to help in any way that our multi-platinum selling home is able. Because I probably love you.

INTENTIONED

I teared up the other day listening to a friend talk about how his girlfriend was secretly planning a trip for him. He saw an email or something that tipped him off and we chatted for over an hour about how incredible that was. It's not even that the trip was a big deal, it is. But, It was more about how she was planning it around a brewery he really digs. Going through the effort of setting up a cool date around things she knew he loved. That's huge. And honestly, pretty rare. I love seeing people give freely. I love watching the excitement of planning something special for someone you love and the receipt of that love. It's all just this magical ball of amazing within the human experience.
I've been seeing a new obsession with what people deserve for their efforts lately. Whether within relationships or work or passion projects, it feels as though everyone is pushing the same line:

If they don't appreciate you, drop them.
I get it. I really do. We live in a weird time of selfish survivalism. Really, the people telling you to drop someone that doesn't appreciate you are trying to protect the fragile hearts we all carry. The idea being, that when we are unfulfilled or underappreciated in our own circles, we should hop into a circle that allows us to feel accepted and to grow.
But, I don't know if this is the right way to approach it. I've been thinking alot about conditioned versus intentioned giving.
"If they don't appreciate you, drop them" Is a prime example of conditioned action. And while it's certainly not the highest on the hierarchy, I think it's a factor in the slow crumbling of our ability to interact with and love each other.
At risk of sounding like a philosophy major that won't pause long enough in my diatribe to take your coffee order, I want to simplify the differences I see between conditional and intentional giving. I think it makes sense to focus on a romantic context, but this really applies anywhere.
You like a girl, right? She's that one you dreamed about before you even knew you liked girls. That sort of show stopping, oh my god, there must be a soul inside me because it matches so perfectly with hers, kind of girl.
You take her coffee, buy her flowers, ask her on dates and buy her food. You both travel to beautiful places and get lost in each other's adoring company. Or so it felt.

But the girl really just wanted a few months of free meals and company while she waited for her ex boyfriend to get out of prison. And now, you sit alone in a booth, in a poetically drab diner, or on a beach somewhere, analyzing everything you did wrong over the last thousand dollars or so of courtship.

She used you, right? Used you to fill the vacuum left by someone else and further, gave you nothing in return.

That hurts, right? And you screwed up.

But you didn't. You only screwed up if your actions were conditional.

"I buy you coffee, you be my girlfriend. I pay for dinner, you kiss me goodnight."

Or whatever. And conditional action, while incredibly common, leaves everyone feeling worse. It's an exchange, and insofar as exchanges commonly work, someone will always feel shorted.

But if you look at those months and that investment of time and energy and money. The emotional capital wasn't a drunken savings dump into DogeCoin because your cousin swore it would go to a dollar, but rather a reflection of your character. The humanity inside of us.

Intentioned giving is bringing her coffee because you want to impress her, date her, have like 12 kids with her.

I don't know what you look for in a partner. Maybe it's 12 kids.

But you want her to see that you care. And you did that. Intentionally and not conditionally.

With intention, it's not that the rejection and misplaced effort doesn't hurt, it does. It's that it matters less because the goal was focused on things you can control rather than a strange scale of effort that so many people attempt to keep in balance throughout their lives and personal relationships.

When we focus on our own shit and the pieces that we can effectually change, we free up that mathematical fatigue of who did what and how much that was worth and are able to simply *give*.

I've been told alot that I'm too easy to take advantage of. That I give my time or talent away too easily and freely.

That can be true in a professional context, but with my friends or with anyone I might be chasing romantically at the moment, it's simply how I choose to show love. And to steal a phrase from the very polarizing, Gary Vee, "You can't take advantage of somebody who's given with no expectation."

I want to act in the way I expect everyone to act. It's cliche, "Be the change", I know, but I want more people to stop expecting a return on their personal investments and instead choose to live in a way that's reflective of their heart and what they want from the world at large.

I wanna be the guy that you know will help you move a mattress, or lay tile, or watch your kid, or fix your computer without an expectation of a return because I genuinely believe that everyone would be better off if we just stopped acting so transactionally. See, now I've morphed from a philosophy major to a socialist stoner, but I'm still a barista not making your coffee.

Sorry.

I hope you look at your own actions and measure them against conditional or intentional giving. And if you've been conditional for a while, maybe try and reshape your thought process inward rather than outward. It doesn't matter if she loves you or not. Bring her a damn coffee and keep pouring out love. Eventually, someone out there will be doing the same thing and you'll be much better prepared to receive it and give it back in kind. And really, that's why we are all here, right? An endless exchange of energy that hopefully results in a positive impact. That's just loving unconditionally. Thanks for reading.

I definitely love you.

THANKS

I owe a great deal to a great number of people. I'd love to act as though I'm the product of my own git and bad attitude but it just isn't true.
Thanks firstly to the Kickstarter supporters.
Taryn Spurrier has known me most of my adult life and has seen me with more hair and less charm than I currently have now. She's a fantastic friend and amazing mom.
Machelle Farrar is an artist who supports every single human that she meets. Her heart is kind and she has brought a genuine smile to the face of one of my best friends recently. I'm so thankful for her.
Andrew Brandt forced me to write about him for money. This is a cry for help. Read his books I guess, they still won't make him any more likable.
Rachael Suffield was an absolute joy to meet and drink coffee with. Her life is fascinating and so is she and I'm so

thankful she decided to support this project.

Talon and Stephanie Meeks have been constant in a way so few people are. They share me with everyone, and encourage me and boost me up in ways I struggle to articulate fully. I appreciate them both so much and their enthusiasm over my projects has been the driving force behind writing books and the music. Thank you.

Erika Munden is a creative gem and a wonderful human. She's a fantastic mother to three amazing kids and I feel so honored to have been able to interview them for this book. Thank you so much.

Adrian Amiro-Wilson is theater weird. Her heart is so kind it doesn't really make sense to me. Hers is a joy that fills up a room and I'm absolutely blown away by her artistic talent. I even have a painting she did of me in my home. Because I am conceited.

Jocelyn Williams is a poet herself and a damned good one. She's a fantastic human and I respect her deeply for her dedication to books and black clothing.

Megan Stutz is a joy. So is her dog. They are both amazing and I'm better for having met them. She has an infectious smile you should hope sincerely that you one day see.

Haley Hotchkiss was a stranger that I found out is a neighbor and is now a fantastic friend. She is genuine and kind and I cannot believe we live so close. I'm very lucky to know her.

Christian Enevoldsen was a formative friend and has known me longer than anyone here aside from family. He saw me at my very least likable (middle school) and somehow we are still friends.

Teysha and Matt are the kind of couple I want to be. I set them up. Just gotta throw that in. Teysha is kind and caring and wonderful conversation. She has dramatically changed my best friend's life and it's been in the absolute best sort of way. I can see how deeply you love him and I'm just so damn happy. Matt has been one of my very best friends in a lifetime that has been full of fantastic people. I can never truly repay him for the enormous impact he has had on my life and my heart. But hopefully that Bumble profile was a start.

Presley Peters is supportive and kind and has a fantastic smile that encourages even assholes like me to smile back. Thank you.

Buster is an incredible friend who gives the best whiskey recommendations and is some of my favorite conversation. I miss him and feel bad for not being as good at texting him as he is me.

Jordan Bailey is creative and talented and wonderful. Thanks for supporting my bullshit.

Emily Backus is one of the coolest people I've never met. I promise she is cooler than you. She tends bar in south texas and even if we never actually spoke in person, I consider you a great friend and I'm glad to know you.

My grandparents Mimi and Pawpaw have been a rock upon whom I can rely always. They are patient and kind and love me more profoundly than most anyone. I am so terribly lucky to have them in my life.

Andrew Monroe is many things, most of them good. He remains the most trustworthy person I know. He is more of a man than I will ever be. Talks with him are always motivational and he has been my confidant and trusted best friend forever.

Tyler and Bethany are dearly missed. I wish they were closer, but more pointedly, wish I lived closer to them.

Kansas is much better than Texas. I mean that. With my whole chest. Come at me cowboys.

Morgan is my very favorite human to gossip with and she lives a life of adventurous enthusiasm I try desperately but always fail to match. If you see her and buy her a drink you can have a friend for life who will improve your life or at the very least, make it more interesting.

Matthew is my cousin with perhaps the kindest heart. He is genuine and cares for literally everyone and I have always admired the way he works so hard to make people feel seen and heard.

Huge thanks to Angela Workman, Ryan McSwain, Nicki Csenge, Jaime, and finally Jennifer Gonzalez. You all made this book work and I deeply appreciate you and your support. Thank you.

Thank you to Amanda Richardson who was the very first person to read my early draft of this book. She is an incredible friend and a crazy talented artist that I hope to meet someday.

I also want to thank my daughter. I hope she never reads this book because of its obviously questionable subject matter. But I also want the world to know that without her brightness, my whole universe would collapse. She is my everything and I didn't fully grasp that phrase before I held her for the first time ten years ago in a hospital as a scared 25 year old musician who desperately needed to grow up. I hope everyday that she finds joy and spreads her kindness and that I can live in a way that makes her proud to call me "dad". I love you Hazel Mae.

There are a ton of other people I would love to list but I'm not going to because none of them paid me. See? Success went to my head. I'm an asshole now. I mean, MORE of an asshole.

Thanks for reading.

LEAVE A REVIEW

Reviews help other people see this book and read all the sad shit I wrote. If you feel like helping please share the book or leave a review on Amazon or Goodreads. Or both if you're especially generous. Thanks.

You can see more of my work at thatporterfield.com

I Am Not In A Good Place

www.ingramcontent.com/pod-product-compliance
Lightning Source LLC
Chambersburg PA
CBHW030302100526
44590CB00012B/490